ADVENTURES IN PARENTING

How

RESPONDING,

PREVENTING,

MONITORING,

MENTORING,

and

MODELING

Can Help

You Be a

Successful

Parent

National Institute of
Child Health and
Human Development

National Institutes
of Health

Table of contents

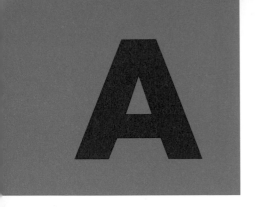

Adventures in parenting

Have you heard the latest advice about parenting?

Of course you have. From experts to other parents, people are always ready to give you parenting advice. Parenting tips, parents' survival guides, dos, don'ts, shoulds, and shouldn'ts—new ones come out every day.

But with so much information available, how can anyone figure out what *really* works? How do you know whose advice to follow? Isn't parenting just common sense anyway? How can the experts know what it's like to be a parent in a *real* house?

What's a parent to do?

Try RPM3—a no-frills approach to parenting from the National Institute of Child Health and Human Development (NICHD).

For over 30 years, the NICHD has conducted and supported research in parenting and child development. We've talked to experts, parents, and children. We've collected statistics, identified myths, and tested suggestions. The result is RPM3.

Parents do matter.

The RPM3 guidelines aren't meant to be just another parenting "how to," telling you what to do. Instead, RPM3 separates the useful information from the not-so-useful so that you can make your own decisions about parenting. RPM3 does more than tell stories about what people *think* about parenting, it incorporates 30 years of NICHD research to tell you what really works.

RPM3 confirms something that you already know: parents *do* matter. *You* matter. Read on to find out just how much...

The first section of this booklet explains each item in RPM3, **responding, preventing, monitoring, mentoring,** and **modeling,** in more detail. These lessons describe how RPM3 can help you make daily decisions about parenting. The remaining sections of the booklet give examples of how some parents have used the lessons of RPM3 with their own children.

As you read, you will notice numbers, like [1] or [7] next to certain words. These numbers relate to the research that supports an idea or concept, listed on the **References** page. These references give you more information about NICHD parenting research.

So where do we start?

The first thing you need to know is that there are no perfect parents. Parenting isn't all-or-nothing. Successes *and* mistakes are part of being a parent. Start to think about the type of parent you want to be. RPM3 offers research-based guidelines for being:

- **An *effective* parent**
  Your words and actions influence your child the way you want them to.

- **A *consistent* parent**
  You follow similar principles or practices in your words and actions.

- **An *active* parent**
  You participate in your child's life.

- **An *attentive* parent**
  You pay attention to your child's life and observe what goes on.

RPM3

stands for:

Responding to your child in an appropriate manner.

Preventing risky behavior or problems before they arise.

Monitoring your child's contact with his or her surrounding world.

Mentoring your child to support and encourage desired behaviors.

Modeling your own behavior to provide a consistent, positive example for your child.

By including responding, preventing, monitoring, mentoring, and modeling in your day-to-day parenting activities, you can become a more effective, consistent, active, and attentive parent.

Once you have learned about each RPM3 guideline, go to the section that describes your child's age to see how some parents use these guidelines in their everyday parenting. Think about steps you can take to use these guidelines and ideas in your own day-to-day parenting.

Being a more effective, consistent, active, and attentive parent is a choice that only you can make.

Keep in mind...

As you learn about the RPM3 guidelines and read the examples, remember that responding, preventing, monitoring, mentoring, and modeling have their place in parenting every child—including those children with special or different needs.

All children—be they mentally challenged, mentally gifted, physically challenged, physically gifted, or some combination of these—can benefit from the guidelines in RPM3. The children described in the booklet's examples might be in wheelchairs; they could have leukemia or asthma; they may take college level courses; or they might be in special classes for kids with attention deficit disorder.

The stories don't specifically mention these traits because all kids need day-to-day parenting, including those in special situations. The guidelines presented in RPM3 focus on how to handle day-to-day parenting choices, in which a child's abilities or disabilities are not the most important factors. The booklet's examples also apply to families of any culture, religion, living arrangement, economic status, and size. They address situations that all families experience, even if the specific family details are slightly different.

Let's begin by learning the lessons that RPM3 has to teach, starting with the **R—Responding to your child in an appropriate manner.**

Responding to your child in an appropriate manner

This guideline may seem obvious, but responding is more than just giving your child attention. The words are actually saying two different things: **1)** make sure you're *responding* to your child, not reacting; and **2)** make sure your response is *appropriate*, not overblown or out-of-proportion, too casual or minimal, or too late.

Are you reacting or responding to your child?

Many parents *react* to their children. That is, they answer with the first word, feeling, or action that comes to mind. It's a normal thing to do, especially with all the other things people do every day.

When you react, you aren't making a decision about what outcome you want from an event or action. Even more than that, if you react, you can't *choose* the best way to reach the outcome you want.

Responding to your child means that you take a moment to think about what is really going on before you speak, feel, or act. Responding is much harder than reacting because it takes more time and effort. The time that you take between looking at the event and acting, speaking, or feeling is vital to your relationship with your child. That time, whether it be a few seconds, five minutes, or a day or two, allows you to see things more clearly, in terms of what is happening right now and what you want to happen in the long-run.

> The time that you take between looking at the event and acting, speaking, or feeling is vital to your relationship with your child.

What is an appropriate response?

An appropriate response is one that fits the situation. Both your child's age and the specific facts of the occasion are important in deciding what a fitting response is. For example, a fitting response for a baby who is crying differs from a fitting response for a four-year-old or a 10-year-old who is crying. A fitting response for an instance in which a child is running depends on whether that child is running into a busy street or running to the swing set on the playground. Your child's physical or emotional needs may also shape your decision about a fitting response.

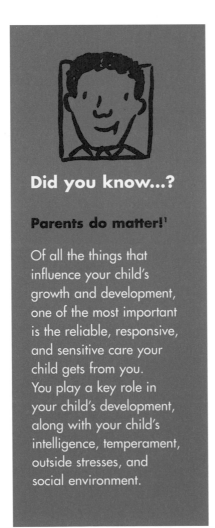

Did you know...?

Parents do matter![1]

Of all the things that influence your child's growth and development, one of the most important is the reliable, responsive, and sensitive care your child gets from you. You play a key role in your child's development, along with your child's intelligence, temperament, outside stresses, and social environment.

Responding to your child in an appropriate manner allows you to:

- **Think about all the options before you make a decision.** This will help you choose the best way to get from the current situation to the outcome that you want. By taking time to see a problem from many sides, for instance, you are more likely to choose the most fitting response. For situations that happen often, your well-thought-out response can become almost automatic, like picking up a crying baby.

- **Answer some basic questions:** Do your words get across what you are trying to say? Do your actions match your words? Are your emotions getting in the way of your decision-making? Do you know the reasons for your child's actions or behavior?

- **Consider previous, similar events and recall how you handled them.**

  You can remind your child of these other times and their outcomes, to show that you are really thinking about your decision. You can use your past experiences to judge the current situation, decide the outcome you want, and figure out how to reach that outcome.

- **Be a more consistent parent.**

  Your child will know that you are not making decisions based on whim, especially if you explain how you made your choice. Your child will be more likely to come to you with questions or problems if he or she has some idea of what to expect from you. Warm, concerned, and sensitive responses will also increase the likelihood of your child coming to you with questions or problems. Remember that consistent parenting does not mean inflexible parenting.

Did you know...?

Parents have a profound influence on children from the beginning of their children's lives.[2]

As a parent, you can have close contact with your child from the time he or she is small. That type of contact builds trust; with trust comes commitment. Parents who are committed to their child's well-being can have a very positive effect on their child.

- **Offer an example of how to make thoughtful decisions.**

  As your child gets older, he or she will know your decision-making process and will appreciate the time you take. Your child might even pattern him or herself after you.

- **Build a solid but flexible bond of trust between you and your child.**

  A solid bond holds up to tough situations; a flexible bond survives the changes in your child and in your relationship with your child that are certain to occur.

Now you can either go to the examples, or read on to learn the **P** in RPM3.

Preventing risky behavior or problems before they arise

Seems easy enough. You "childproof" your house to make sure your crawling baby or toddler can't get into the cleaning products or electrical outlets. You catch your eight-year-old jumping on the bed and make her stop. You make your 12-year old wear his helmet when he rides his bike, no matter how "dumb" he thinks it makes him look.

But prevention goes beyond just saying "no" or "stop." There are two parts to prevention: **1)** Spotting possible problems; and **2)** Knowing how to work through the problem. Let's look at each one a little closer.

Spotting possible problems

Consider these methods for spotting problems before they turn into full-blown crises:

- **Be actively involved in your child's life.**
  This is important for all parents, no matter what the living arrangements. Knowing how your child usually thinks, feels, and acts will help you to notice when things begin to change. Some changes are part of your child's growing up, but others could be signs of trouble.

- **Set realistic limits and enforce them consistently.**
  Be selective with your limits, by putting boundaries on the most important behaviors your child is engaged in. Make sure you and your child can "see" a limit clearly. If your child goes beyond the limit, deal with him or her in similar ways for similar situations. If you decide to punish your child, use the most effective methods, like restriction or time-outs. You could also make your child correct or make up for

the outcome of his or her actions; make sure the harshness of the punishment fits your child's "crime." As your child learns how limits work and what happens when he or she goes past those limits, he or she will trust you to be fair.

- **Create healthy ways for your child to express emotions.**

Much "acting out" stems from children not knowing how to handle their emotions. Feelings can be so intense that usual methods of expressing them don't work. Or, because feelings like anger or sadness are viewed as "bad," your child may not want to express them openly. Encourage your child to express emotions in a healthy and positive way; let your child see you doing things to deal with your own emotions. Once these feelings are less powerful, talk to your child about how he or she feels and why. Make sure your child knows that all emotions are part of the person that he or she is, not just the "good" or happy ones. Once your child knows his or her range of emotions, he or she can start to learn how to handle them.

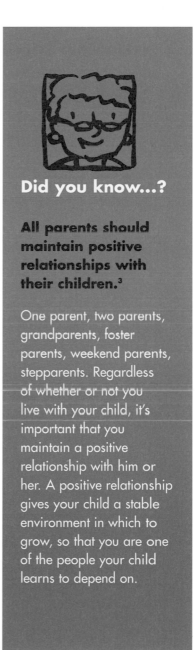

Did you know...?

All parents should maintain positive relationships with their children.[3]

One parent, two parents, grandparents, foster parents, weekend parents, stepparents. Regardless of whether or not you live with your child, it's important that you maintain a positive relationship with him or her. A positive relationship gives your child a stable environment in which to grow, so that you are one of the people your child learns to depend on.

Knowing how to work through the problem

Because problems are quite different, how you solve them also differs. To solve tough problems, you may need more complex methods. Keep these things in mind when trying to solve a problem:

- **Know that you are not alone.**
  Talk to other parents or a trusted friend or relative. Some of them might be dealing with or have dealt with similar things. They may have ideas on how to solve a problem in a way you haven't thought of. Or, they might share your feelings, which can also be a comfort.

- **Admit when a problem is bigger than you can handle alone or requires special expertise.**
  No one expects you to solve every problem your family has by yourself. Some problems are just too big to handle alone, not because you're a "bad" parent, but simply because of the nature of the problem. Be realistic about what you can and can't do on your own.

- **Get outside help, if needed.**
  There will be times when you just won't know how to help your child; other times, you truly won't be able to help your child. That's okay; someone else may know how to help. Use all the resources you have to solve a problem, including getting outside help when you need it. Remember that it's not important how a problem is solved, just that it is.

Where can I go for parenting help?

- Other parents
- Family members and relatives
- Friends
- Pediatricians
- School nurses and counselors
- Social workers and agencies
- Psychologists and psychiatrists
- Pastors, priests, rabbis, and ministers
- Community groups
- Support and self-help groups

If you'd like, turn to the section that matches your child's age to read more about how some parents have included **preventing** in their daily parenting routine. Or you can read on to learn about the **M3** in **RPM3**.

The **M3** in RPM3 describes three complex, but central principles of parenting: **monitoring, mentoring,** and **modeling**. Many people are confused by these words because they seem similar, but they are really very different. It might be easier to understand these ideas if you think of them this way:

- **Being a monitor** means that you pay careful attention to your child and his or her surroundings, especially his or her groups of friends and peers and in getting used to school.

- **Being a mentor** means that you actively help your child learn more about him or herself, how the world works, and his or her role in that world. As a mentor, you will also support your child as he or she learns.

- **Being a model** means that you use your own words and actions as examples that show your beliefs, values, and attitudes in action for your child on a daily basis.

Now let's look at each one more closely. **Monitoring** your child seems straightforward, so let's start there.

Monitoring your child's contact with his or her surrounding world

Do you need to be a superhero with x-ray vision and eyes in the back of your head to be a careful monitor? Of course not. You don't need to be with your child every minute of every day, either. Being a careful monitor combines asking questions and paying attention, with making decisions, setting limits, and encouraging your child's positive choices when you aren't there.

When your child is young, monitoring seems easy because you are the one making most of the decisions. You decide who cares for your child; you decide what your child watches or listens to; you decide who your child plays with. If something or someone comes in contact with your child, you're usually one of the first to know.

Things may change as your child gets older, especially after school begins and into the pre-teen and teen years. As kids begin to learn about their own personalities, they sometimes clash with their parents' personalities. A parent's ability to actively monitor is often one of the first things to suffer from this clash.

Parents need to monitor their children's comings and goings through every age and stage of growth.

Being a careful monitor combines asking questions and paying attention, with making decisions and setting limits.

Being an active monitor can be as simple as answering some basic questions:

- **Who** is your child with?
- **What** do you know about the person(s) your child is with?
- **Where** is your child?
- **What** is your child doing?
- **When** will your child be home/leaving?
- **How** is your child getting there/home?

You won't always have detailed answers to these questions, but it's important to know most of the answers, most of the time.

You may also want to keep these things in mind when being an active monitor:

- **Open the lines of communication when your child is young and keep those lines open.**

  It seems obvious, but honest communication is crucial. When your child is young, talk openly about things you do when you aren't with your child; then ask your child what he or she does during those times. As your child gets older, keep up this type of communication. Both you and your child have to take part in open, two-way communication.

- **Tell your child what thoughts and ideals you value and why.**

  For instance, if being respectful to adults is an ideal you want your child to have, tell him or her; even more importantly, tell him or her *why* you think it's important. Don't assume that your child knows your reasons for valuing one practice or way of behaving over another.

With a little effort from you, your child might surround him or herself with friends whose values, interests, and behaviors will be "pluses" in your child's life.

- **Know what your child is watching, reading, playing, or listening to.**

  Because TV, movies, video games, the Internet, and music are such a large part of many of our lives, they can have a huge influence on kids. Be sure you know what your child's influences are. You can't help your child make positive choices if you don't know what web sites he or she visits or what he or she reads, listens to, watches, or plays.

- **Know the people your child spends time with.**

  Because you can't be with your child all the time, you should know who is with your child when you're not. Friends have a big influence on your child, from pre-school well into adulthood. Much of the time, this influence is positive, but not always. With a little effort from you, your child might surround him or herself with friends whose values, interests, and behaviors will be "pluses" in your child's life. Your child also spends a lot of time with his or her teachers. Teachers play a vital role in your child's development and overall well-being, so get to know your child's teachers, too.

- **Give direction without being rigid.**

  In some cases, *not* being allowed to do something only makes your child want to do it more. Is the answer just plain "no" or does it depend on the circumstances? "Yes, but only if..." is a useful option when making decisions.

  To find out how some parents use **monitoring** in their daily parenting practices, turn to the section of this booklet that relates to your child's age. Or you can read on to learn about **mentoring**.

A special note to those of you with pre-teens or teenagers[4,5]

Keep in mind that even if you're the most careful monitor, your child may have friends and interests that you don't understand or don't approve of. You may not like the music she listens to, or the clothes he wears, or the group she "hangs out" with. Some of these feelings are a regular part of the relationship between children and adults. Before you take away the music or forbid your child to see that friend, ask yourself this question:

Is this (person, music, TV show) a *destructive* influence?

In other words, is your child hurting anyone or being hurt by what he or she is doing, listening to, wearing, or who he or she is spending time with? If the answer is "no," you may want to think before you act, perhaps giving your child some leeway. It's likely that taking music away, not letting your child watch a certain show, or barring your child from spending time with a friend will create a conflict between you and your child. Make sure that the issue is important enough to insist upon. Think about whether your actions will help or hurt your relationship with your child, or whether your actions are necessary for your child to develop healthy attitudes and behaviors. You may decide that setting a volume limit for the radio is better than having a fight about your child's choice of music.

Being your child's *mentor* can keep your child from being hurt by encouraging him or her to act in reasonable ways. Now let's think about **mentoring**.

Mentoring your child to support and encourage desired behaviors

When you were growing up, did you have a special person your life who did things with you, gave you advice, or was a good listener? This person may have been a relative or friend of the family who was older than you. If so, then you had a mentor.

Since the early 1980s, formal mentoring programs that pair children with caring mentors have been highly successful. Mentoring, whether an informal relationship or a formal program, has a focused goal: guiding children through adolescence so they can become happy, healthy adults.

You may know that all children need mentors, but did you know that parents make great mentors?

Mentors help kids reach their full potential, which includes mistakes and tears, as well as successes and smiles.

What does it mean to be a mentor?

A mentor is someone who provides support, guidance, friendship, and respect to a child.

Sounds great. But what does *that* mean?

Being a mentor is like being a coach of a sports team. A caring coach sees the strengths and weaknesses of each player and tries to build those strengths and lessen those weaknesses. In practice, coaches stand back and watch the action, giving advice on what the players should do next, but knowing that the players make their own game-time decisions.

Coaches honestly point out things that can be done better and praise things that are done well. Coaches listen to their players and earn players' trust. They give their players a place to turn when things get tough.

Mentors do the same things: develop a child's strengths; share a child's interests; offer advice and support; give praise; listen; be a friend. Mentors help kids to reach their full potential, which includes mistakes and tears, as well as successes and smiles. Mentors know that small failures often precede major successes; knowing this fact, they encourage kids to keep trying because those successes are right around the corner.

What can I do to be a mentor?

There is no magic wand that turns people into caring mentors. Just spending time with your child helps you become a mentor. You can do ordinary things with your child, like going grocery shopping together; you can do special things with your child, like going to a museum or a concert together. The important part is that you do things *together,* which includes communicating with one another.

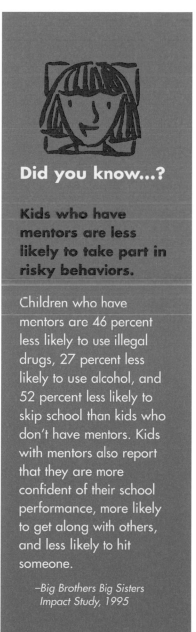

Did you know...?

Kids who have mentors are less likely to take part in risky behaviors.

Children who have mentors are 46 percent less likely to use illegal drugs, 27 percent less likely to use alcohol, and 52 percent less likely to skip school than kids who don't have mentors. Kids with mentors also report that they are more confident of their school performance, more likely to get along with others, and less likely to hit someone.

–Big Brothers Big Sisters Impact Study, 1995

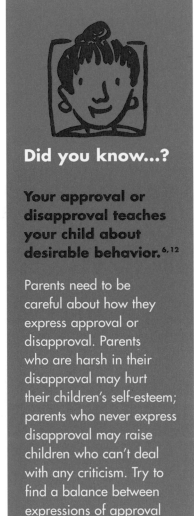

Did you know...?

Your approval or disapproval teaches your child about desirable behavior.[6,12]

Parents need to be careful about how they express approval or disapproval. Parents who are harsh in their disapproval may hurt their children's self-esteem; parents who never express disapproval may raise children who can't deal with any criticism. Try to find a balance between expressions of approval and disapproval. Be consistent in your rewards and punishments.

You may want to keep these things in mind as you think about being a mentor:

- **Be honest about your own strengths and weaknesses.**

  If you know the answer to a question, say so; if you don't, say so. To build a trusting, but real, relationship with your child, you only have to be human. All humans make mistakes; you have, and your child will, too. Your child can benefit from hearing about your mistakes, including what you thought before you made them, how your thoughts changed after you made them, and how you changed your thoughts or behaviors to avoid them in the future. A child who thinks his or her parent is perfect builds expectations that parents can't possibly live up to.

- **Respect your child's thoughts and opinions without judging them.**

  Even if you don't agree with your child, make it clear that you want to know what his or her thoughts are, without the threat of punishment.
  If your child is afraid of being punished,

he or she may stop sharing things entirely. Let different points–of–view co–exist for a while; they will allow your child to think more about an issue. Remember that there is an important difference between, "I disagree with you," and "You're wrong."

- **Support your child's interests and strengths, but don't force things.**

  Kids spend their childhood trying to figure out who they are, how the world works, and how they fit into that world. Make sure your child has enough room to explore. If your child has no interest in an activity or topic, don't push. Your child will soon begin to dread the "forced activity" and will find ways to get out of doing it.

- **Introduce your child to things that you like to do.**

  This is a useful way for your child to learn more about you. It's sometimes hard for kids to picture their parents doing things that other people do, like playing an instrument, volunteering at a nursing home, watching movies, playing a sport, or knowing about art. If your child sees you doing these things, you become more of a "regular person," rather than "just a parent."

To read more about how some parents fit **mentoring** into their daily parenting activities, turn to the section of the booklet that relates to your child's age. Or, read on to learn about **modeling**.

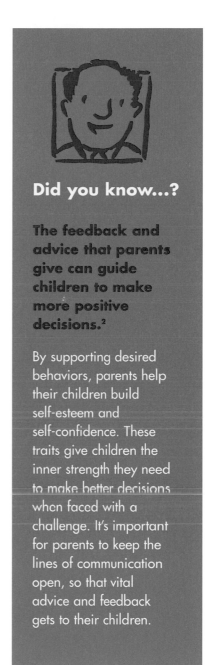

Did you know...?

The feedback and advice that parents give can guide children to make more positive decisions.[2]

By supporting desired behaviors, parents help their children build self-esteem and self-confidence. These traits give children the inner strength they need to make better decisions when faced with a challenge. It's important for parents to keep the lines of communication open, so that vital advice and feedback gets to their children.

Mentoring gives kids the support they need to become the people they are meant to be. But what about you? Are you the person you want to be? Take some time to think about becoming a better **model** for your child.

Modeling your own behavior to provide a consistent, positive example for your child

When I grow up, I want to be just like you.

Has your child ever said this to you?

It's a bittersweet statement for a parent to hear. On the one hand, it's touching to have your child look up to you in this way; on the other, being a role model comes with great responsibility.

Children learn as much, if not more from your actions as they do from your words.

Role models come in all shapes and sizes; they do all kinds of jobs; they come from any country or city. Some children view athletes as their role models; other children look up to authors or scientists. And, believe it or not, many children see their parents as role models.

All too often, parenting behavior is guided by adults reacting to their own childhoods; that is, many parents think: I don't *ever* want to be like my parents; or it was good enough for me, so it's good enough for my kids. Remember that reacting instead of responding prevents you from making decisions that can change the outcome of a situation. To be a more effective, consistent, active, and attentive parent, it's best to focus on your children and their lives.

Does this mean that you have to be perfect so your child will grow up to be perfect, too? Of course not. No one is perfect. But, you do need to figure out what kind of example you are setting for your child.

You may want to be the kind of role model who does the following:

- **Do as you say _and_ say as you do.**

  Children want to *act* like their role models, not just talk like them. Children learn as much, if not more from your actions as they do from your words. Don't just tell your child to call home if he or she is going to be late; make sure that *you* call home when you know you're going to be late. Don't just tell your child not to shout at you; don't shout at your child or at others. This kind of consistency helps your child form reliable patterns of the relationship between attitudes and actions.

- **Show respect for other people, including your child.**

  For many children, the word *respect* is hard to understand. It's not something they can touch or feel, but it's still a very important concept. To help your child learn about respect, you may want to point out when you are being respectful. For instance, when your child starts to pick out his or her own clothes, you can show respect for those choices. Tell your child, "That wouldn't have been my choice, but I respect your decision to wear that plaid shirt with those striped pants."

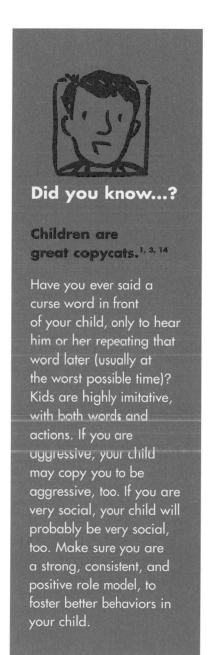

Did you know...?

Children are great copycats.[1, 3, 14]

Have you ever said a curse word in front of your child, only to hear him or her repeating that word later (usually at the worst possible time)? Kids are highly imitative, with both words and actions. If you are aggressive, your child may copy you to be aggressive, too. If you are very social, your child will probably be very social, too. Make sure you are a strong, consistent, and positive role model, to foster better behaviors in your child.

Did you know...?

How parents act in their relationships with one another has a significant impact on child development.[2]

Regardless of the living arrangements, parents should consider their children when dealing with each other. Your child sees how you work through everyday issues and uses your interactions as the basis for his or her own behavior in relationships. The next time you interact with your spouse, ex-spouse, or significant other, ask yourself whether or not you are providing a positive example for your child. Do you want your child to act the same way you are acting with that person or another person? If not, you may want to reconsider your behavior.

- **Be honest with your child about how you are feeling.**

  Adults get confused about emotions all the time, so it's no surprise that children might get confused, too. For instance, you might have a short temper after a really stressful day at work, but your child might think you are angry with him or her. If you find yourself acting differently than you usually do, explain to your child that he or she isn't to blame for your change in "typical" behavior; your child can even help you by lightening your mood or altering your attitude. You can prevent a lot of hurt feelings and confusion by being honest with your child about your own emotions.

- **Make sure your child knows that being angry does not mean, "not loving."**

  Disagreements and arguments are a normal part of most relationships. But many children can't separate love from anger; they assume that if you yell at them, then you don't love them anymore. Even if you think your child has a solid grasp of emotions, you may want to be specific about this point. Otherwise, you run the risk of having your child think he or she is not loved every time you have a disagreement. Most of all, be alert to changes in your child's emotions so you can "coach" your child through moments of anger or sadness without brushing-off the emotion or ignoring it.

- **Pinpoint things that you wouldn't want your child's role model to do, and make sure you aren't doing them.**

For instance, suppose your child views a sports player as his or her role model. If you found out that player used illegal drugs or was verbally or physically abusive to others, would you still want your child to look up to that person? Probably not. Now apply that same standard to your own actions. If you don't want your child to smoke, then you should not smoke. If you want your child to be on time for school, make sure you are on time for work and other meetings. If you don't want your child to use curse words, then don't use those words in front of your child. Reviewing your own conduct means being honest with yourself, about yourself. You may need to make some changes in how you act, but both you and your child will benefit in the end.

Did you know...?

How you feel affects your child.[6,9]

Your child tunes into your thoughts, feelings, and attitudes. He or she can sense how you feel about something, even if your words say that you are feeling something different. So a negative reaction or outburst from your child may not be without reason. It could be your child's way of telling you how you feel.

Now what should I do?

Now that you know about RPM3, it's time to put these ideas into action. Find the section that matches your child's age and read through it to see how parents like you have brought RPM3 into their lives. Take some time to think about the examples, answer the related questions, and make decisions about how RPM3 can fit into your style of parenting on a daily basis.

Responding to your child in an appropriate manner

The example below will give you a better idea of what it means to respond to your child in an appropriate manner. As you read, think about these questions:

- **Is the parent in the story reacting or responding?**
- **Is her response appropriate to the child's age?**
- **Is her response appropriate to the situation?**
- **How might you respond to your child in the same situation?**

Caroline and Abby (Age 1 ½)[7]

What's the Story? Abby spends the day at a day care center while Caroline is at work; Caroline drops her off at 7:30 a.m. and returns for her at 5:30 p.m. When they get home in the evening, Caroline gets dinner ready while Abby sits in her high chair. Caroline keeps the chair turned so that Abby is facing her while she cooks, so that they can watch, smile at, and talk to each other.

It takes Caroline a little longer to make dinner because she often stops to play peek-a-boo or bends down to talk to Abby at her eye-level. They have their own conversations, in which Abby "talks" and Caroline "answers." If Abby is cranky or upset, Caroline uses this time to calm her down and figure out why she's being fussy. Caroline has found many ways to keep Abby calm as a result of this dinnertime contact, that are also helpful when the two are out of the house running errands.

Caroline Says: That time with Abby, while I'm cooking, is really important to me. I can connect with her, get to know her better. I look forward to it, even after a full day at work. It has helped me to learn what she likes and what she doesn't.

What's the Point? Caroline is right about the importance of her dinner-time contact with Abby. Research shows that children need to spend positive, engaging, playful time with their parents each day.[1] This "special" time allows parents to bond with children, to learn what makes them smile or laugh, what kinds of noises they respond to, how they respond, and what feelings their toddlers' "words" convey. Early and consistent communication between parent and child is essential to forming attachments, as well as to building better emotional, intellectual, and social development. Setting aside this kind of time every day also lets kids learn about their parents. They can tune in to facial expressions, body language, and tone-of-voice to know their caretakers better.

In a perfect world, you could spend all day, every day with your child, never missing a meal or a moment of togetherness. In the real world, however, this is often not the case. Regardless of how you manage it, you should try to make time for this kind of interaction with your child every day. The specifics of where, how, or when you spend time with your child aren't as important as the actual time you spend with your child.

If your child won't sit in a highchair for very long, put some toys on the floor and let your child play there while you're in the kitchen. If you're driving here and there, talk to your child as you drive, pointing out things you see or singing songs. If you see your child in the mornings, get into a routine for getting dressed together so that you can interact with him or her. You can also include the other people in your family in this time together, so that your child becomes more comfortable in the family setting. The important part is getting to know your child and letting your child get to know you.

Preventing risky behaviors
or problems before they arise

The next story shows how you might prevent problems before they arise. As you read, think about these questions:

- **Are the parents active in their child's life?**
- **Is the problem bigger than the parents can handle alone?**
- **Should the parents seek outside help?**
- **How might you handle a similar situation with your child?**

Molly, Ron, and Stefanie (Age 4 weeks)[7]

What's the Story? Stefanie is Molly and Ron's first child. Before Stefanie was born, the couple planned for Molly to take three months of parental leave from her job after the baby was born. Now, only a few weeks after Stefanie's birth, Molly is having problems caring for the baby.

Ron Says: Molly just doesn't seem to want to be with Stefanie. There are times when I walk in the door and hear Stef wailing because she's hungry or needs to be changed; then I find that Molly is sitting in the next room crying, too.

Sometimes she forgets to feed Stef—how can you *forget* to feed a baby? I'm worried that Stefanie isn't getting get the attention she needs during the day. I mean, sometimes Molly doesn't even get dressed during the day. I wish I knew how to make things better for all of us.

Molly Says: I know that a lot of women do the mom thing every day, but I'm just not as good at it as they are. Sometimes, it's like nothing I do is enough for her. I try holding her, rocking her, feeding her, playing with her, but she still cries. I can't do anything right.

What's the Point? While it's true that millions of women "do the mom thing" every day, none of them would say it's easy. Being a mother takes a lot of getting used to; in fact, *being a parent* takes a lot of getting used to.

But it sounds like Molly is going through more than getting used to being a new mom. For nearly 10 percent of women who are pregnant or give birth, the weight of being a new mom is doubled by post-partum depression, an illness that results from hormonal changes related to pregnancy and giving birth.[15] Women with post-partum depression need more help than their spouses or partners can give, more than they can give themselves, actually. For many women like Molly, professional treatment from a psychiatrist or other mental health professional is the best way to beat the so-called "baby blues."

If any parent, no matter what their gender is, finds it hard to relate with their child in a playful, positive way, then they should seek outside help immediately. Molly and Ron might want to talk to her obstetrician about how they are feeling and how things are going. The doctor may have some ideas that could help, like hiring a babysitter a few days each week, or having each parent take "alone time" during the week. The doctor might also refer them to a psychiatrist or another mental health professional so they can get help through counseling and medication.

Having a baby changes every part of parents' lives, including their relationship to each other. Many times, one or both parents have a hard time adjusting to all the changes. Parents should know that their emotional health has a big impact on their child's emotional health. Getting help right away is the best way to ensure the child's and the parents' well-being.

Monitoring your child's contact with his or her surroundings

How can you be a careful monitor? This next example may help you decide. As you read, think about these questions:

- **Is the parent being an active monitor?**
- **Is she being flexible?**
- **Does she know who the child is spending time with or what the child is doing when she's not there?**
- **How might you handle a similar situation with your child?**

Maria and Luis (Age 9 Months)

What's the Story? Maria is taking her son, Luis, to his first morning of day care. She signed up with the center several months ago, because it had the best location, and visited the center once during the last month. Maria knows that state law requires that day care centers have a three-to-one ratio for children under one year of age—that is, one day care staff person will care for her Luis and only two other children his age. She feels better knowing he will get more personalized care throughout the day. When Maria calls the center during the day to see how Luis is doing, the staff person only replies with, "He's fine." When she picks up Luis after work, the staff person doesn't say very much about his day and seems to shuffle mother and child out the door. Maria notices that Luis is kind of cranky and wonders what his day was really like.

Maria Says: It took me a long time to decide whether or not I was going to put Luis into day care. It's even harder now to know whether I made the right decision. It's frustrating not knowing what is going on in my baby's day. How can I know that he's being cared for when I can't be there?

What's the Point? The best way to make sure Luis gets the care Maria wants him to have is to know as much about the day care center and the people who work there as possible. Maria is her son's best defense against poor care, but only if she is actively monitoring his surroundings. Some day care centers provide a daily diary of every child's day—when they fed the baby, when they changed the baby, who played with the baby, and what they played with. If Maria had asked more questions about the daily routine of the center when she went for her visit, she could've found out whether the center offered that type of report. If she knew the center did not keep a diary for each child, she could have made other arrangements for Luis at a center that did offer the daily report.

If you decide to place your child into day care, learn as much as you can about the center and its workers before you take your child there. Decide what features you *must* have in a day care center. You may want your child to get a lot of one-on-one attention; or you may want your child to be around kids the same age so that he or she can build social skills. You may want a report of what happens to your child throughout the day. Remember, though, that more attentive care often costs more than the alternatives.

Once you know what you want, find a place that meets *all* your needs. Visit the center before signing any papers or giving any money. If you can, make one or two unannounced visits to the center, so that you can see how well it runs on a normal day. Contact your local licensing agency to make sure the center has all of the required licenses and permits; find out if there have been any problems reported for the center or its employees. You can also ask the day care center staff for references, which allows you to check their work histories. The more work you do upfront, the more pleased you will be with the care your child receives.

Mentoring your child to support and encourage desired behaviors

Now look at this example of parents being mentors. As you read, think about these questions:

- **Are these parents being thoughtful mentors?**
- **Are they being honest about themselves?**
- **Are they judging their child?**
- **Are the parents supporting the child's interest or forcing the child to develop one?**
- **How might you handle a similar situation with your child?**

LiMing, Yeung, and Chang (Age 3)[4]

What's the Story? Reading is a big part of LiMing and Yeung's lives. They both enjoy reading and do it as often as they can, usually reading at night instead of watching TV. When Chang was born, they asked their health care provider about reading to him. When should they start reading to him? When will he start to read on his own? What is the best way for them to help him learn to read? Now they try to read to Chang every night before he goes to sleep.

LiMing Says: Ever since I was young, I've always liked to read. When Yeung and I got together, reading was one of the things we shared. It seemed only natural for us to extend our passion for reading to Chang.

Yeung Says: I think Chang likes reading, too. He helps turn the pages, points to the pictures he recognizes, and chatters. He knows what is going to happen next and tells me when I've skipped something. He's beginning to recognize the letters and their sounds. He has his favorite books and wants to hear them again and again.

What's the Point? LiMing and Yeung have given a lot of thought to being Chang's mentors. By reading to Chang, they introduced him to one of their interests. They encourage him to choose his own stories and to interact with them and with the book while they're reading. As he gets older, Chang will know that his parents read a great deal. He may decide to join his parents in their hobby.

They may not know it, but LiMing and Yeung are also helping Chang build his reading skills. Studies show that, in the US, more than 50 percent of children are read to by a family member every day.[8] In these studies, family reading is related to better reading comprehension and greater school success. Reading to your child also improves his or her **emergent literacy**—the knowledge that the words printed in books have meaning. One of the key factors in emergent literacy is being able to recognize letters of the alphabet; other factors include knowing the sounds of letters at the beginning and end of words. Reading to your child improves these skills, which can improve your child's chances for school success.

Modeling your own behavior to provide a consistent, positive example for your child

Take a look at this example of a parent being a model. As you read, think about these questions:

- **Is this parent being a positive role model?**
- **Do his words and actions match?**
- **Is he being honest with himself about his own actions?**
- **How might you handle a similar situation with your child?**

Marco and Sabby (Age 2) [1,14]

What's the Story? Marco cares for his son Sabby on the weekends. Now that Sabby is walking and talking, Marco has to watch him more closely so that he doesn't get into trouble. A few weekends ago, Sabby stuck a metal bookmark into an electrical outlet that Marco leaves uncovered so that he can plug in the coffee maker in the morning. Sabby blew out all the fuses in the house, but luckily was not hurt. Despite Marco's scolding, Sabby still goes near the outlet when he gets the chance.

Marco Says: I don't know why he keeps doing it. I've told him "no"; I've said "bad"; I've told him he could get really hurt. But he still goes over to that outlet.

What's the Point? Sabby may still show interest in the outlet because Marco's words don't match his actions. Marco tells Sabby, "no"; but Sabby sees Marco put the coffee maker plug into the outlet. Sabby doesn't know the difference between the plug that's supposed to go in the outlet and other metal objects that shouldn't.

While Sabby is at this age, Marco needs to cover the outlet with a safety cover anytime the coffee maker is not plugged in. Then Sabby won't have the chance to get into it. When Sabby is a little older (three or so), Marco can explain the details of safe materials, dangerous materials, and electrical outlets.

He could also tell Sabby that only grownups are allowed to touch electric outlets. It seems as though Marco is trying to get this across by saying, "no" or "bad," but he only assumes that Sabby knows what he means. Kids, especially young children, will copy what they see even if they don't fully understand it. Sabby's action is a dangerous behavior that could cause him serious harm. Marco needs to take immediate action to ensure Sabby's safety.

Responding to your child in an appropriate manner

The story below will give you a better idea of what it means to respond to your child in an appropriate manner. As you read, think about these questions:

- **Is the parent in the story reacting or responding?**
- **Is his response appropriate to the child's age?**
- **Is his response appropriate to the situation?**
- **How might you respond to your child in the same situation?**

Raj and Amira (Age 8)[3]

What's the Story? When Raj decided to be a stay-at-home dad, his daughter was three. He set up a routine for their days, so that Amira would always know what was going to happen and what was expected of her. When she started kindergarten, Raj changed the routine to fit in the school-related activities, such as doing homework and reading together. Now that Amira's eight, she's more interested in doing things with her schoolmates and neighbors, such as playing at her friends' houses or getting involved in a community sports team. But Raj will not let her take part in these activities because he wants to keep her on the same schedule. When Raj says "No" to Amira, she is disappointed and withdraws from him.

Raj Says: Amira has to get back on our schedule. It's worked so well all this time. She has been up until 8:30 p.m. every night this week. Once we get back on track, things will be better.

What's the Point? Raj is right about the need for solid routines and schedules, but he forgot about the need to be flexible. Younger children do very well with a steady schedule; it allows them to become relaxed in their worlds and learn what their worlds expect from them.

But, schedules also need to adapt to normal changes that occur as kids get older. Amira is just starting to build friendships, a key feature in normal social growth. By now, her regular bedtime should probably be 8:00 p.m., or 8:30 p.m., depending on how much sleep she needs. As Amira matures, she'll need to balance school, home, health, and her friends. Raj can help her create and maintain that balance, if he shows her what it means to be flexible.

When he started the schedule, Raj had Amira's best interests in mind. With some minor changes, Raj's schedule can co-exist with Amira's growth in a way that suits them both.

Preventing risky behavior or problems before they arise

The next example shows how you can prevent problems before they arise. As you read, ask yourself these questions:

- **Is the parent active in the child's life?**
- **Are the limits involved realistic?**
- **Are the limits being enforced consistently?**
- **How might you handle a similar situation with your child?**

Andre and Calvin (Age 4)[1,4,10]

What's the Story? Andre arranged his work schedule so that he can spend all day Saturday with his son, Calvin, every week. After lunch on their Saturdays together, Andre and Calvin spend time cleaning up Calvin's room. "What's our goal?" Andre asks Calvin. "No toys on the floor." Calvin answers.

Andre lets Calvin play while they clean, but within certain limits so that Calvin keeps their goal in sight. Andre uses an egg timer to let Calvin know when it's playtime and when it's time to clean up. He sets it for short intervals, like 10 or 15 minutes, so that Calvin can play a little and then clean up a little. Calvin knows that when he hears the bell, he has to pick up at least three toys and put them away. Andre sets and re-sets the timer in front of Calvin and leaves it in a place where they can both see it (and hear it). By the end of the afternoon, all of Calvin's toys are picked up off the floor.

Andre Says: Calvin needs to learn about goals and limits so he understands moderation. I use the timer because he can see, hear, and touch it. Even though I'm the one setting the time limit, the timer "enforces" it. This keeps him from getting upset with me.

What's the Point?

Setting goals and limits for your child is one way he or she can learn about boundaries. A child Calvin's age has an easier time learning about a goal when it's something he or she can see, so it's clear when the job is finished. Andre's choice of limit (playing versus cleaning) is also realistic; Calvin is capable of picking up all the toys from the floor. The timer offers a constant before-and-after way for Calvin to know when he's reached the limit. Before the bell goes off, this will happen; after the bell rings, that will happen. The child learns that after the bell, after mom counts to three, or after dad counts to 10, something happens. If the child reaches the goal, then praise and kindness follow; if not, some type of outcome for going beyond the limit follows, be it a scolding, a punishment, or another response appropriate to the situation.

Using the timer is a good idea, especially when dealing with a child as young as Calvin. It is a dependable way for Andre to enforce the limits. Because Andre uses similar times, like 10 minutes or five minutes, Calvin gets used to the practice. And, the bell always rings, which provides more order for Calvin.

Monitoring your child's contact with his or her surroundings

How can you be a careful monitor? This next example may help you decide. As you read, think about these questions:

- **Is the caretaker being an active monitor?**
- **Is it clear why a value or behavior is desirable or undesirable?**
- **Is the caretaker being flexible?**
- **Is the child's behavior destructive?**
- **How might you handle a similar situation with your child?**

Keisha and Tyrell (Age 7) [1, 11]

What's the Story? Keisha, who is 20, has been taking care of her brother Tyrell since their mother died last year. She lets Tyrell watch TV while she gets dinner ready; after dinner, the TV goes off. Keisha usually heads to the kitchen to start dinner after she watches the first few minutes of a show with Tyrell. Lately, though, she's noticed a change in the kind of shows Tyrell watches. Instead of his regular programs, Tyrell now watches a show that Keisha hasn't seen before. One evening, she asks Tyrell how he knows about the show. He explains that he heard about it at school.

Keisha Says: I didn't see very much of it at first, but it didn't seem like the kind of show a seven-year-old would watch. It wasn't a cartoon; it didn't have any puppets or animals. So, I asked him not to watch it until I had a chance to see the whole show. I told him he could either watch one of the shows I had already seen, or he could turn the TV off and play. He went off to play by

himself. It's a good thing, too, because the next day I watched that show— I couldn't believe it! Almost every line had something about fighting and getting even. There was a lot of talk about sex, too. I know Tyrell will be exposed to violence in the real world, but I don't want him to start acting like the characters on that show. I don't want him to be ignorant about sex, either, but I want to be the one to teach him about it. He is simply not allowed to watch that show.

What's the Point? Keisha handled this case like a seasoned monitor. First, she watched the first few minutes of TV with Tyrell, to see what he was watching. She also paid attention to the kind of shows that Tyrell usually watched, which made it easier for her to notice a change. After she saw the change, she asked Tyrell how he heard about the new show. And, she watched the show, to make sure that it was okay for Tyrell to watch.

As it turned out, the show wasn't something she wanted Tyrell to see, so he is no longer allowed to watch it.

To really make her point clear, Keisha might want to talk to Tyrell about why she doesn't want him to watch the show. It may not seem important for Keisha to explain her reasons now because Tyrell is so young, but it's a good habit for her to get into for when he gets older. It may also help Tyrell to make better choices about the shows he watches in the future.

Finding some viewing alternatives for Tyrell would also help Keisha make her point. Keisha can rent videotaped movies for Tyrell with messages that she feels are positive. Many of the programs on public television stations are also smart choices, although many are aimed at kids a little younger than Tyrell.

Giving him the option of not watching TV at all is also effective. Oftentimes, kids aren't really interested in watching TV, but they can't think of anything else to do. Simply telling them to turn off the TV and do something else can be a source for arguments. Offering a choice between watching TV and doing something your child usually enjoys allows your child to make his or her own decision. In many cases, your child will opt for playing or coloring. Your child will appreciate your suggestion and your support of his or her ability to make decisions.

Mentoring your child to support and encourage desired behaviors

Now check out this example of parents being mentors. As you read, think about these questions:

- **Is the parent being a thoughtful mentor?**
- **Is she being honest with herself?**
- **Is she judging her child?**
- **Is the parent developing the child's interest or forcing the child to develop an interest?**
- **How might you handle a similar situation with your child?**

Irit and Ari (Age 9)

What's the Story? Ari is a very outgoing boy, who joins many clubs and groups at once. At school, he signs up for scouting troops, sports teams, music lessons; anything that he hasn't tried is interesting to him. As a result, Ari leaves a lot of things unfinished, dropping out of one thing to pursue another. Although Irit encourages her son to try new things, she is worried about him trying too many things at once.

Irit Says: He doesn't stay focused on any one thing long enough to know if he likes it. He may be a gifted artist, or a graceful athlete, or a natural leader. But he never stays with one thing long enough to really learn it and grow in it. I'm glad he has so many interests, but he doesn't seem to know when to stop.

What's the Point? As his mentor, Irit should be honest with Ari about her concerns. She is proud of all the things Ari does, but she thinks he should try to expand one or two of those interests. Irit may want to set some rules to limit the number of clubs and sports Ari can do over a given time. Ari can decide for himself which thing (or things) he wants to pursue. Irit may want to get involved in some of these things as well, by being a scout leader or bringing snacks to games and practices.

Ari also needs to learn that finishing things is just as important as trying new things. Here, again, Irit can set up some rules for Ari. For instance, Irit could limit the lessons or hobbies that cost money. If Ari chooses to take a dance class that costs money and lasts for six weeks, then he has to attend all six weeks of the dance class, even if he loses interest after the first week. Or, she may limit him to only one activity that carries a cost for a certain time. Because most hobbies carry some cost, Ari can't do as many things at once. He then has to focus on only a few things at a time.

It's also essential that Irit explain her actions to Ari. If she limits his hobbies without telling him why, Ari may think that his mother doesn't want him to do anything or have any fun. Showing support is one of the main jobs of a mentor.

By explaining her decision, Irit can show her support while keeping things under control. She should also make it clear to Ari that he doesn't have to be an expert at everything. Irit can give examples of things she started but eventually stopped because she either lost interest in them, or they weren't as rewarding as other activities. Ari needs to know that it's acceptable to do things because you want to, even if you aren't the best at them.

Modeling your own behavior to provide a consistent, positive example for your child

Take a look at this example of parents as models. As you read, consider these questions:

- **Are these parents being positive role models?**
- **Do the parents' words and actions match?**
- **Are the parents being respectful of others? Of their children?**
- **Are these parents being honest with themselves about their own actions?**
- **How might you handle a similar situation with your child?**

Andy, Kristi, Pat, and Jason (Age 7)[2,3,4]

What's the Story? Kristi and Andy split up nearly five years ago, when their son Jason was two. Andy has remarried, and Kristi and Jason have been living with Pat for the last three years. Andy tries to be very active in his son's life, which is a source of conflict for Kristi. She can't let go of her anger toward Andy and makes sour comments about him in front of Jason. When Andy comes to pick up his son, Kristi usually starts an argument with him, about child support or the timing of visits. Pat tries to buffer Kristi's anger, but feels that her attitude is bad for all of them, especially Jason.

Pat Says: I'm not saying that she should forgive and forget her time with Andy. But at the very least she should curb her anger when Jason's around. The poor kid is stuck in the middle. Jason loves his mom _and_ his dad; he should love _both_ his parents. I try to stay out of it most of the time, because it's an issue that is best kept between Kristi and Andy, but her attitude fills our home with such negativity that I sometimes have to change the subject for Jason's sake. And for my own sake.

Kristi Says: No one really knows what Andy is like, except me. He's the one who left _me_ with a toddler and no means of support, without a second thought. Pat has no idea what I went through. I'm just getting Jason ready for the hurt and disappointment that his father is sure to bring. It's only a matter of time before he leaves Jason, too. Pat just doesn't know.

Andy Says: Kristi is out-of-control. I thought she had finally moved on when she moved in with Pat, but I guess not. You can see how upset Jason gets when she starts saying those things; it's written all over his face. I can tell it makes Pat uncomfortable, too. I've tried to make it clear that arguing in front of Jason is not acceptable to me. But Kristi never stops. Even though I try to explain to Jason that his mom and my arguments aren't his fault, I know he's hurt by the whole situation.

What's the Point? It's hard for any child to hear awful things about his or her parent day after day; it's even worse when the other parent is the one saying those awful things. Jason is left having to choose between his mother and his father. It's an awful position for a child to be placed in.

Despite her claims that she is trying to prepare Jason for disappointment, Kristi's actions are more hurtful to him than helpful. It makes sense that she wants to protect Jason, but her actions focus on protecting herself. She needs to see that things are no longer about her and Andy, but that Jason is what's most important. Jason needs to be allowed to develop his own relationship with each parent, one that doesn't involve the other. He will make his own decisions about his father and mother and how active he wants them to be in his life as he gets older. Kristi's actions may force Jason to limit his time with her later in his life.

4-10 YEARS

Andy's point about not arguing in front of Jason is also important. Again, the issue is between Kristi and Andy; Jason should not be involved, even as a bystander. It's painful and confusing for children to hear their parents argue. They often blame themselves for their parents' words and actions, thinking that if they behaved better or did better in school, then their parents would get along. Both Andy and Kristi need to reassure Jason that their fighting is not his fault. If Kristi is unable or unwilling to help Andy convey this to Jason, maybe Andy can enlist Pat's help. Regardless of who reinforces the idea, it's vital for Jason to know that his parents have problems with each other, not with him.

Responding to your child in an appropriate manner

The example below will give you a better idea of what it means to respond to your child in an appropriate manner. As you read, think about these questions:

- **Are the parents in the story reacting or responding?**
- **Is their response appropriate to the child's age?**
- **Is their response appropriate to the situation?**
- **How might you respond to your child in the same situation?**

Nancy, Akira, and Koji (Age 11) [4,6]

What's the Story? Koji is an active, bright, 11-year-old boy. He plays soccer in the area league, likes computer games, and sleeps over at his friends' houses. He also "hates" anything related to school, especially homework, and goes out of his way to avoid all things linked to school. His parents, Nancy and Akira, know that Koji is avoiding his homework and often punish him to try to change his attitude and behavior. The result is a daily battle.

Nancy Says: We've tried everything. We tell him, "Do your homework or no TV." Or, "Do your homework or you can't go to your friend's house." We've sent him to his room, taken away his games, even sent him to tutors. Nothing works.

Akira Says: He just doesn't understand the importance of good study habits. If he develops good study habits now, while he's young, he'll have an easier time in the older grades. I don't know why he doesn't see that. He doesn't have any discipline.

What's the Point? Koji might not be able to see his parents' point-of-view because they haven't told him <u>why</u> they want him to do his homework. To them, the reasons are clear: they want Koji to build good study habits now so that he will do well in high school. Even more than that, they want to instill a sense of discipline in Koji, so that he learns how to start <u>and</u> finish things. For Nancy and Akira, these ideas don't need to be explained.

For Koji, discipline and study habits are just words his parents use when they talk about school. But he probably doesn't really know what these words mean. His parents need to explain these things in a way that makes them more concrete or real for Koji. Also, because he only 11, Koji doesn't think in terms of his future. He can't see how the things he does now affect the things he'll do when he's 20. (In fact, he thinks 20 is old!) Koji can't yet see himself in the future, beyond the idea that his body will get bigger. His parents need to help him to envision his possible future selves so that he recognizes the link between present action and future consequence.

Another thing Koji's parents should think about is his "history" with school. Has Koji always disliked school or is this a recent change in his attitude? How are his grades now as compared to his grades in the past? How are his friends doing in school? Has there been a change in their attitudes as well? Koji could be slightly more advanced than some of his classmates; if that's the case, he might be bored. Or the opposite may be true; Koji may be frustrated because he doesn't understand what he's trying to learn, so maybe he's just giving up. If Koji's friends are showing some of the same changes in behavior and attitude, maybe the friends are influencing each other into not liking school. Nancy and Akira should talk to Koji's teachers and to his friends' parents to try to figure out when his change in attitude started and what was happening around him at that time.

Nancy and Akira may also want to build family "homework time" into their nightly routine. By setting aside time for Koji to do homework, while one or both of his parents are in the room reading or doing some other type of work, Nancy and Akira can help Koji turn an idea like discipline into an action.

It's much easier for children to know _what_ you're doing if they know _why_ you're doing it. Explaining your reasons for doing or not doing things gets across your values more effectively by showing those values in action. If you support your actions with reasons, you also give your child his or her best example of how to make an informed choice. This practice also brings more order into your child's world, by showing a starting point (your value/reason) and an end point (your action/choice) for an event.

11-14 YEARS

Preventing risky behavior or problems before they arise

The next example shows how you can prevent problems before they arise. As you read, ask yourself these questions:

- **Is the parent active in the child's life?**
- **Are the limits involved realistic?**
- **Is the problem bigger than the parent can handle alone?**
- **Should the parent seek outside help?**
- **How might you handle a similar situation with your child?**

Janice and Christopher (Age 14) [2,5,6]

What's the Story? Lately, Christopher has been spending a lot of time in his bedroom with the door closed. When Janice knocks on his door, he rarely answers her; when she enters the room, he is lying on his bed listening to his radio with his headphones on. "Can't you KNOCK?" he yells. When Janice asks him what he's listening to, he says "Nothing." Christopher has gotten four after-school detentions in the last month, mostly for getting into fights and arguments. Janice knows that Christopher shouts at her and at his younger sister more often than he used to, but she's not sure why he's so angry or how to help him.

Janice Says: He's always kept to himself, but I've never seen him like this. The littlest thing can make him explode. It doesn't make sense. His grades are fine; he does his chores; he dresses the same. He's just so angry. What if he hits someone? What if his yelling changes into punching? What can I do? I'm really worried about him.

Christopher Says: I wish she would lay off! She's always asking stupid questions, like "What are you listening to?" or "What's wrong with *you*?" She probably thinks I'm doing drugs or that I worship the devil or something. *Nothing* is wrong with me. I just want to be left alone.

What's the Point? Christopher may be trying to keep his mother out of his life, or he might just want time by himself to think. In his mind, there's no point in answering her questions because she couldn't possibly know what he is going through, thinking, or feeling. Many kids Christopher's age feel this way and go to extremes to prevent their parents from knowing anything about them. After a while, many parents stop trying to know their kids because their feelings get so hurt when their kids reject them. Sadly, both the parents and the kids end up feeling very alone.

While Christopher may keep pushing her away, Janice needs to let him know she cares about him. She can't _make_ him talk to her; she can't force him to be her friend. But she can show Christopher that she loves him, she is interested in him, and she isn't going away no matter how mean he is to her. By not forcing the issue, she also shows him that she respects his privacy.

Janice should also seek out new and different ways to spend time with Christopher. Being involved in the same project or going somewhere "cool" together is a more natural way to reconnect and redefine their roles with one another. It also allows their relationship to accommodate the new, young-adult Christopher and his interests as things continue to change.

Janice needs to let Christopher know what is acceptable and what is not, when it comes to how he treats her and his younger sister. Janice should make it clear that he must treat her with respect and speak to her and his sister without raising his voice. Christopher may try to isolate himself even more as he gets older, so this issue is worth the struggle because it sets a minimum level of contact for family and son at this stage of their lives. Janice accepts that Christopher doesn't want to share his life with her, but she will not accept him being disrespectful to her or her daughter.

Of greater concern is Christopher's level of anger and how he deals with it. His yelling and fighting is a new thing that may be a sign of trouble. Anger is a tough emotion for many kids to handle because our culture frowns on expressing anger. Most of the contact kids and adults have with anger is seeing it expressed in its most extreme form: violence. Sadly, violence is the only way that many people know to deal with their anger.

Janice may want to enlist some outside help to teach Christopher how to deal with his anger in a more positive way. Many community centers, health care professionals, school counselors, and teen groups teach classes on how to manage anger. They show people how to control anger and how to express it without hurting themselves or others. Another option for Janice is to get Christopher involved in a healthy outlet for his anger. Running, boxing, writing in a journal, playing the drums, even crying are ways to channel anger so it's more constructive than destructive. Having an outlet for anger and other emotions keeps them from building up inside, which also prevents them from bursting out in harmful or violent ways.

Monitoring your child's contact with his or her surroundings

How can you be a careful monitor? This next example may help you decide. As you read, think about these questions:

- **Are these grandparents being active monitors?**
- **Is it clear why a value or behavior is desirable or undesirable?**
- **Are these grandparents being flexible?**
- **Is the child's behavior destructive?**
- **How might you handle a similar situation with your child?**

Sam, Esther, and Rachel (Age 13)[2,3]

What's the Story? Rachel has been living with her grandparents, Sam and Esther, since she was a baby. Until recently, Sam and Esther agreed on the values and behaviors that they wanted to teach their granddaughter. But now that Rachel is a teenager, they don't agree on issues that involve her.

Sam Says: I know that I agreed to let Rachel wear makeup, but I'm still not comfortable with the idea. She looks like a 30-year-old, not a 13-year-old. Plus, isn't makeup just the beginning? Next thing you know, she'll want to go places with her friends without chaperones. Then what?

Esther Says: If we tell her she can't dress the way she wants or wear makeup when she wants, she'll just start doing it anyway and lying to us about it. She asked me if she could start wearing makeup to school. I discussed it with Sam and he agreed, so Rachel and I went out and bought what she wanted together. Then I showed her how to apply the makeup without putting on too

53

much. Wearing makeup *is* just the beginning of Rachel's process of becoming who she wants to be. But I want to make sure that Sam and I are a part of that process from the beginning.

What's the Point? It's only natural for Sam to try to protect his granddaughter, but being strict with her may have the opposite effect. If Rachel feels that her grandparents aren't willing to listen to her needs and wants, she may decide not to get their input at all. Cutting off communication with her grandparents leaves Rachel at greater risk for getting hurt, having problems, and feeling pressured.

By going with Rachel to buy makeup and showing her how to apply it, Esther and Sam are providing guidance without being rigid. While wearing makeup may seem like a small issue, Esther and Sam are setting a solid example for making choices as Rachel gets older. Not only are they aware of what Rachel is doing, but they are also keeping the lines of communication open. The manner in which they handle this situation will let Rachel know whether her grandparents support her growing up. With that knowledge, Rachel is more likely to talk to her grandparents about other important issues, like boys and dating, which can help prevent future problems.

Esther and Sam decided together that Rachel's wearing makeup wasn't an issue worth fighting over. If Sam has doubts about that decision, he needs to discuss them with Esther so they can find a compromise that is agreeable to both of them. If Sam's doubts are not about Rachel wearing makeup, but stem from his worries about other things, like going out with friends, dating or curfews, then he and Esther need to talk about those issues while letting their initial decision about makeup stand.

Mentoring your child to encourage and support desired behaviors

Now consider this example of parents being mentors.
As you read, think about these questions:

- **Are these parents being thoughtful mentors?**
- **Are the parents being honest about themselves?**
- **Are they judging their child?**
- **How might you handle a similar situation with your child?**

Alexander, Masha, and Greg (Age 12) [1,3,13]

What's the Story? Greg has been having a hard time with school lately. He's always been an able student, getting good grades and doing other activities, like playing his guitar. But since he started sixth grade, he's been having trouble, mostly in his math class. Even though he does all his homework and studies for the tests, he just isn't doing as well as he used to. In spite of help he gets from his stepmother, Masha, Greg's grade hasn't improved. To try and take his mind off his grade, Greg has been playing his guitar at night after working with Masha on his homework. When Greg brought home a "C" in math on his report card, his father, Alexander, punished him by taking his guitar away.

Alexander Says: He isn't applying himself. When I was in school, I wasn't allowed to do any after-school activities. I had to come home from school and study and that's it. And I never got a "C." If he spent less time playing that guitar and more time on his studies, he could get better grades.

11-14 YEARS

Masha Says: I don't know why Alexander won't listen to me. I've tried to talk to him about this, about the fact that Greg is trying really hard, but he just won't listen. I told him I didn't agree with punishing Greg for his grade, but he did it any way. To Alexander, the effort isn't important, just the end result. Besides, how will Greg learn to balance school and other things if he's not allowed to do any other things?

What's the Point? Alexander may want to rethink his actions in this case. First, he isn't listening to Masha. Parenting is about talking, listening, and most of all, compromising. These concepts apply regardless of the living arrangements. Parents need to work together to make decisions about the children they are raising. How Alexander interacts with Masha influences how Greg views his stepmother and how he treats her. As Greg's mentor, Alexander should respect Masha's opinion and her input into parenting decisions. Otherwise, Greg may think it's acceptable to ignore Masha's opinions and input as well.

Secondly, Alexander isn't recognizing Greg's efforts. Greg chose to work very hard to try and do well in the class; he also chose not to quit and not to blame anyone else for his grade. These choices show strength, maturity, and determination. As Greg's mentor, Alexander should value Greg's hard work and let Greg know that he values it. Alexander should also support

Greg's decision to keep trying in spite of the outcome. By putting so much weight on the end result (the grade), Alexander could prevent Greg from learning that it's not whether you win or lose, but how you play the game. His persistence and effort should be applauded.

Without knowing it, Alexander is also sending a message that he doesn't believe in Greg's ability to do well. He doesn't expect Greg to be able to handle both playing guitar and school; he expects Greg to fail. What parents expect from their kids affects how much their kids achieve. With his father's message in mind, Greg may assume that he is going to fail without even trying. Even though Alexander is trying to drive Greg to do better, this hidden message could lead Greg to give up instead.

Masha's point about balance is a good one, too. Kids (and adults) have to learn how to fit many things into their lives. Limiting Greg's activities also limits his practice of doing many things at once by making him do only one thing at a time. Even Alexander will agree that life usually gives us a number of challenges at once. This is a lesson that Greg is better off learning when he is younger.

Kids aren't always going to succeed; they won't always get the best grades; they won't win every race. Sometimes, your child may need help from someone other than you, like from a tutor or a special teacher. As your child's mentor, you need to support your child's desire to try and his or her effort to succeed, no matter what the outcome.

Modeling your own behavior to provide a consistent, positive example for your child

Take a look at this example of parents as models. As you read, think about these questions:

- **Are these parents being positive role models?**
- **Do the parents' words and actions match?**
- **Are the parents showing respect to others? To their children?**
- **Are these parents being honest with themselves about their own actions?**
- **How might you handle a similar situation with your child?**

Anna, Ignacio, and Tomás (Age 11)[1,2,3,14]

What's the Story? Tomás has been getting into trouble at school. To figure out what the problem might be, Anna and Ignacio met with Tomás' teachers. According to his teachers, Tomás is usually a well-behaved, calm little boy. But when he spends time around some of the girls in the class, he is aggressive and usually more physical, often pushing or pinching them. When questioned, Tomás explained that he is "just goofing around" with the girls and doesn't mean to hurt them. But Tomás is big for his age, the teacher says, and doesn't know how strong he really is. Anna and Ignacio are worried; they tell the teachers that they will talk to their son.

Anna Says: I think I know what he's doing. Ignacio and I are a physical couple. We sometimes tease and wrestle as a way of showing our fondness for each other. In fact, Ignacio has told Tomás that we are "just goofing around" a number of times. Maybe Tomás is starting to notice girls and being physical is how he's showing it.

Ignacio Says: That's silly! Tomás knows that he shouldn't be pushing or hitting the girls. His mother and I tease each other, but it is never as physical as pushing or hitting. Tomás must've gotten this from TV. I think we should punish him by not letting him watch TV for a while. That'll stop this nonsense.

What's the Point? Even though Anna and Ignacio know the context of their playful contact with one another, Tomás does not. Ignacio knows that his and Anna's actions are the result of many years together, their respect for each other, and their love; in his mind, these facts should be clear to Tomás. But Tomás is only 11 and love and respect are only words to him. Tomás is not aware of the time and work that Anna and Ignacio have put into their relationship; he only sees the end result. Tomás thinks that all men and women are playful with each other because that is what he sees every day; if he "likes" a girl he should be playful with her, too.

Tomás also has a limited knowledge of his own body. He grows and changes every day, so he may not know his own strength. What he sees as "goofing around" may actually hurt someone else. Ignacio and Anna's actions never go far enough to hurt, Tomás doesn't have that kind of control over his body yet. He doesn't know when to stop.

Anna and Ignacio need to discuss how they want to handle this situation and find a compromise. Anna may have a point about Tomás and his possible new interest in girls; Ignacio could be correct about the types of TV shows that Tomás is watching. It could be that their son's actions result from a combination of things. By talking over their thoughts and opinions, Anna and Ignacio can come up with a plan of action that is acceptable to both of them.

Ignacio and Anna need to explain to Tomás that how they act with each other is special. It's different from how Tomás should act with other people. They may want to tell Tomás that he shouldn't touch any of the kids in his class for a little while, even if he thinks he is just being playful. These limits will allow Tomás to learn some level of control for his own body. He will also learn what actions are proper, when, and with whom. The process of developing self-control or regulating one's own social behavior is a slow process. In addition to having patience with their son, Anna and Ignacio also need to model more appropriate behaviors for Tomás to learn and adopt in his daily life. These behaviors may include keeping their relationship more private, until Tomás is older and can understand it better.

Remember...

By including the RPM3 guidelines in your day-to-day parenting activities, you can become a more successful parent. RPM3 means:

- **Responding to your child in an appropriate manner**
- **Preventing risky behavior or problems before they arise**
- **Monitoring your child's contact with his or her surroundings**
- **Mentoring your child to support and encourage desired behaviors**
- **Modeling your own behavior to provide a consistent, positive example for your child**

Being a more effective, consistent, active, and attentive parent is a choice that only you can make. Enjoy your adventure!

References

1. L. Alan Sroufe, Ph.D., Professor, Institute of Child Development, University of Minnesota.
2. E. Mark Cummings, Ph.D., Professor, Children and Families Developmental Psychopathology, Department of Psychology, University of Notre Dame. From: Cummings, Davies, & Campbell (In Press). *Developmental Psychopathology and Family Process.* NY: Guilford Publications, Inc.; and Cummings, Goeky-Morey, & Graham (In Press). "Interparental relations as a dimension of parenting." Bristol-Power, Borkowski, & Landesman Ramey (Eds.). *Parenting and the child's world: Multiple influences on intellectual and socio-emotional development.* Hillsdale, NJ: Erlbaum.
3. Kristen Moore, Ph.D., Executive Director, and Tamara Halle, Child Trends, Inc., Washington D.C.
4. John Borkowski, Ph.D., Andrew J. McKenna Family Chair and Professor of Psychology, Department of Psychology, University of Notre Dame.
5. Sharon Ladesman Ramey, Ph.D., Director and Professor, Civitan International Research Center, University of Alabama.
6. Laraine M. Glidden, Ph.D., Division of Human Development, St. Mary's College of Maryland.
7. Geraldine Dawson, Ph.D., Professor of Psychology, Department of Psychology and Center on Human Development and Disability, University of Washington, Seattle.
8. Federal Interagency Forum on Child and Family Statistics, *America's Children: Key National Indicators of Well-Being, 2000.* Federal Interagency Forum on Child and Family Statistics, Washington, D.C.: U.S. Government Printing Office.
9. Cohn and Tronick, *Child Development,* 1983.
10. Rubin, Stewart, and Chen. *Handbook of Parenting, Volume 1,* 1995.
11. Dorr and Rabin, *Handbook of Parenting, Volume 4,* 1995.
12. Edwards, *Handbook of Parenting, Volume 1,* 1995.
13. Stevenson and Lee, *SRCD Monographs,* 1990.
14. Radke-Yarrow et al., *Manual of Child Psychology,* Mussen (ed.), 1983.

Acknowledgements

The NICHD would like to thank the Robert Wood Johnson Foundation for its contributions to the conference *Parenting and the Child's World: Multiple Influences on Intellectual and Socio-economic Development,* which provided the impetus for this publication, and its continued support for this effort. The NICHD would also like to thank the NIH Office of Behavioral and Social Science Research for its support of this publication.

The author would like to thank John Borkowski, PhD, Marie Bristol-Power, PhD, Dana Bynum, and Sharon Landesman-Ramey, PhD, for their dedication and assistance in creating this publication, and Laraine M. Glidden, PhD,. for her keen review of the material. In addition, the author gives a special nod of thanks to the staff of the Public Information and Communications Branch of the NICHD for their patience and careful reviews of the material presented in this publication.

In addition, the author sends her deepest thanks to Margaret Georgiann for her creativity, design expertise, and patience in completing this booklet.